ESSENTIAL DK COMPUTERS

WORD PROCESSING

DESIGNING DOCUMENTS

ABOUT THIS BOOK

Designing Documents is for people with an understanding of the basics of word processing using Microsoft's Word, including opening a document, entering text, and saving a document.

THIS BOOK CONCENTRATES ON THE facilities that Word offers for designing more interesting and professional documents than those produced by using only the default settings that Word provides. These facilities include font selection, customizing and manipulating paragraphs, adding colored borders and backgrounds, using tabs, columns, and lists, and creating your own style sheets.

These features are presented in chapters where related elements are grouped together for an easier understanding of what actions are possible and how to carry them out. These build on previous explanations so your knowledge is developed through a logical sequence.

The chapters and the subsections use a step-by-step approach. Virtually every step is accompanied by an illustration showing how your screen should look at each stage. The screen images are either full-screen or they focus on an important detail that you'll see on your screen. If you work

By using the techniques in this book, you can improve the look of all your Word documents.

through the steps, you'll soon start feeling comfortable that you're learning and making progress.

The book contains several features to help you understand both what is happening on screen and what you need to do. A labeled Word window is included to show the important elements that are used in Word. This is followed by an illustration of the toolbars, at the top of the screen, to help you find your way around these invaluable, but possibly perplexing, controls.

Cross-references are shown in the text as left- or right-hand page icons: ⬑ and ⬏. The page number and the reference are shown at the foot of the page.

In addition to the step-by-step sections of the book, there are also boxes that describe and explain particular features of Word in detail, and tip boxes that provide alternative methods and shortcuts. Finally, at the back of the book, you will find a glossary explaining new terms and a comprehensive index.

ESSENTIAL COMPUTERS

WORD PROCESSING

DESIGNING DOCUMENTS

JOHN WATSON

A Dorling Kindersley Book

Dorling Kindersley
LONDON, NEW YORK, DELHI, SYDNEY,
PARIS, MUNICH, JOHANNESBURG

Produced for Dorling Kindersley Limited by
Design Revolution, Queens Park Villa,
30 West Drive, Brighton, East Sussex BN2 2GE

EDITORIAL DIRECTOR Ian Whitelaw
SENIOR DESIGNER Andy Ashdown
PROJECT EDITOR John Watson
DESIGNER Paul Bowler

MANAGING EDITOR Sharon Lucas
SENIOR MANAGING ART EDITOR Derek Coombes
DTP DESIGNER Sonia Charbonnier
PRODUCTION CONTROLLER Wendy Penn

Published in Great Britain in 2000 by
Dorling Kindersley Limited,
9 Henrietta Street, London WC2E 8PS

2 4 6 8 10 9 7 5 3 1

A CIP catalog record for this book is available from the British Library.

ISBN 0-7513-0996-6

Color reproduced by First Impressions, London
Printed in Italy by Graphicom

For our complete
catalog visit
www.dk.com

CONTENTS

MICROSOFT WORD

Microsoft Word has been around for well over a decade and, with each new release, adds to its reputation as the world's leading word-processing program.

WHAT CAN WORD DO?

The features contained in Word make it one of the most flexible word-processing programs available. Word can be used to write anything from shopping lists to large publications that contain a wide range of features in addition to the main text. These include, illustrations and graphics, charts, tables and graphs, captions, headers and footers, cross references, footnotes, indexes, and glossaries.

Word can correct spelling and grammar, check readability, search for text and replace it, import and sort data, perform calculations, and provide templates for many types of documents from memos to Web pages. The comprehensive and versatile design, formatting, and layout options in Word make it ideal for desktop publishing on almost any scale. In short, there's very little that Word cannot do.

WHAT IS A WORD DOCUMENT?

In its simplest form, a Word document is a sequence of characters that exists in a computer's memory. Using Word, a document can be edited, added to, and given a variety of layouts. Once the document has been created, a large number of actions can be carried out, such as saving, printing, or sending the document as an email.

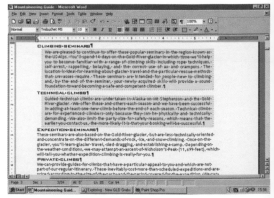

LAUNCHING WORD

Word launches just like any other program running in Windows. With the Windows desktop on screen, you can launch Word as the only program running, or you can run Word alongside other software to exchange data with other applications.

1 LAUNCHING BY THE START MENU

• Place the mouse cursor over the **Start** button on the Taskbar and click with the left mouse button.
• Move the cursor up the pop-up menu until **Programs** is highlighted. A submenu of programs appears to the right.
• Move the cursor down the menu to **Microsoft Word** and left-click again. (If Microsoft Word is missing from the Program menu, it may be under Microsoft Office.)
• The Microsoft Word window opens △.

2 LAUNCHING BY A SHORTCUT

• You may already have a **Shortcut to Word** icon on screen. If so, double-click on the icon.
• The Microsoft Word window opens △.

8 The Word Window

THE WORD WINDOW

At first, Word's document window may look like a space shuttle computer display. However, you'll soon discover that similar commands and actions are neatly grouped together. This "like-with-like" layout helps you quickly understand where you should be looking on the window for what you want. Click and play while you read this.

THE WORD WINDOW

❶ Title bar
❷ Menu bar
Contains the main menus.
❸ Standard toolbar
Buttons for frequent actions.
❹ Formatting toolbar
Main layout options.
❺ Tab selector
Clicking selects type of tab.
❻ Left-indent button
Used to set left-indents.
❼ Ruler
Displays margins and tabs.
❽ Right-indent button
Used to set right-indent.
❾ Insertion point
Shows where typing appears.
❿ Text area
Area for document text.
⓫ Split box
Creates two text panes.
⓬ Scroll-up arrow
Moves up the document.
⓭ Scroll-bar box
Moves text up or down.
⓮ Vertical scroll-bar
Used to move through text.

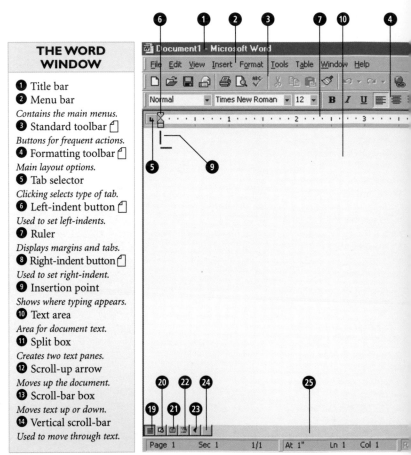

The Word Toolbars 10

Changing the Indent 28

TOOLBAR LAYOUT

If Word doesn't show the Formatting toolbar below the Standard toolbar, first place the cursor over the Formatting toolbar "handle." When the four-headed arrow appears, (right) hold down the mouse button and "drag" the toolbar into position.

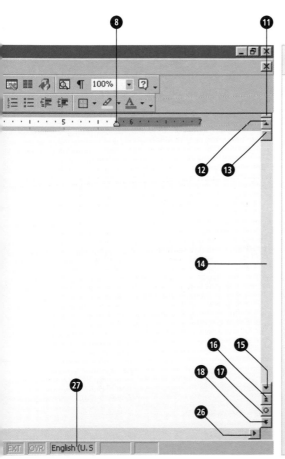

THE WORD WINDOW

15 Scroll-down arrow
Moves down the document.

16 Page-up button
Shows previous page of text.

17 Select browse object
Opens browse options menu.

18 Page-down button
Displays next page of text.

19 Normal view
Default document view.

20 Web layout view
Web-browser page view.

21 Page layout view ⌐
Printed-page view of text.

22 Outline view
Shows document's structure.

23 Left-scroll arrow
Shows the text to the left.

24 Scroll-bar box
Moves text horizontally.

25 Horizontal scroll bar
To view wide documents.

26 Right-scroll arrow
Shows the text to the right.

27 Language
Spelling, thesaurus, and proofing settings.

EXT OVR English (U.S

12 **The chosen view**

THE WORD TOOLBARS

Word provides a range of toolbars where numerous commands and actions are available. The principal toolbars are the Standard toolbar and the Formatting toolbar, which contain the most frequently used features of Word. There are also more than 20 other toolbars available for display. Click on **Tools** in the Menu bar ⬐, move the cursor down to **Customize**, and click the mouse button. The **Customize** dialog box opens. Click the **Toolbars** tab to view the variety of toolbars available.

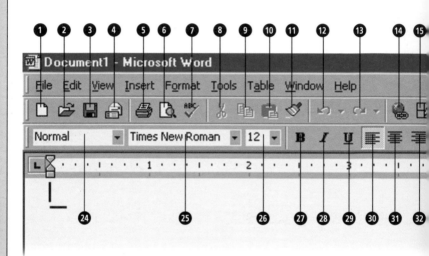

THE STANDARD TOOLBAR

1. New document
2. Open folder or file
3. Save
4. Email
5. Print
6. Print preview
7. Spelling and grammar
8. Cut text
9. Copy text
10. Paste text
11. Format painter 📄
12. Undo action(s)
13. Redo action(s)
14. Insert hyperlink
15. Tables and borders
16. Insert table
17. Insert Excel worksheet
18. Columns ⬐
19. Drawing toolbar
20. Document map
21. Show/hide formatting marks
22. Zoom view of text
23. Microsoft Word help

 Menu bar 8

Using Format Painter 35

 Using Multiple Columns 48

CUSTOMIZING A TOOLBAR

To add a **Close** button to a toolbar, click on the **Commands** tab of the **Customize** box (see left). Place the cursor over the **Close** icon, hold down the mouse button, drag the icon to the toolbar, and release the mouse button.

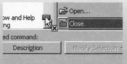

ScreenTips

It isn't necessary to memorize all these buttons. Roll the cursor over a button, wait for a second, and a ScreenTip appears telling you the function of the button.

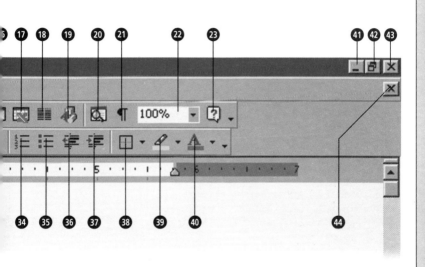

THE FORMATTING TOOLBAR

24 Style selector
25 Font selector
26 Font size selector
27 Bold
28 Italic
29 Underline
30 Left-aligned text
31 Centered text

32 Right-aligned text
33 Justified text
34 Numbered list
35 Bulleted list
36 Decrease indent
37 Increase indent
38 Outside border
39 Highlight color

40 Font color
41 Minimize Word
42 Restore Word
43 Close Word
44 Close document

21 Bold, italic, and underline

22 Aligning Paragraphs

40 Quick lists

WORKING WITH FONTS

There are several different levels of formatting and styling available in Word. This chapter looks at changing the font, resizing it, and changing the spacing and color of the letters.

CHANGING THE FONT

The default font in Microsoft Word is Times New Roman, which is one of the most popular fonts. There are many other fonts available and, while you can use as many fonts as you wish in a document, it is better to use no more than three in any one section. Increasing the number of fonts can have the effect of fragmenting the text and making it look messy, and certain fonts do not look good together.

THE CHOSEN VIEW

Throughout this book it is recommended that you work in Print Layout view, as many of the effects used are only displayed in this view of a document. To do this, click on **View** in the Menu bar and select **Print Layout**, or click on the **Page Layout View** button at the bottom of the screen.

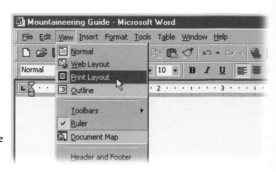

A VARIETY OF FONTS

In the examples of styling and formatting text that are used throughout this book, the text is displayed in a variety of fonts. While Microsoft Word includes a range of the most commonly used fonts, you may not have all the fonts shown here. This will not affect your ability to work your way through the examples, but you will need to choose alternative fonts. An almost limitless number of fonts can be bought from stores or over the Internet.

㉑ Page layout view

1 CREATING THE TEXT

● In the example used here, we are writing a document for a mountaineering company that offers guided expeditions and more.

● Begin by typing their contact details in a new document, and press Enter← at the end of each line with an extra Enter← after the zip code.

● You'll see that when the email address is typed in, Word recognizes it for what it is and automatically shows it in blue.

Email address ●

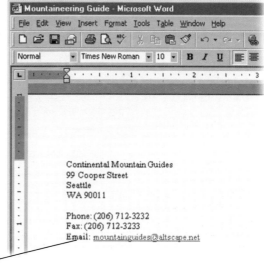

2 SELECTING A NEW FONT

● Although this text is perfectly clear, it lacks any impact. The first change that you can make is to use different fonts to emphasize the different parts of the company's details.

● Highlight the company name, click on **Format** in the Menu bar, and click on **Font** at the top of the drop-down menu.

● The **Font** dialog box now opens. In the **Font:** selection menu, use the scroll bar to move to another font (we have chosen Charlesworth, which has only upper-case letters). The **Preview** panel at the foot of the dialog box shows how the text will appear in your document. Click on **OK**.

● For the rest of the contact details, except for the email address, we are going to use another font. Highlight the text to be selected, open the **Font** dialog box again, and choose another font (we selected BankGothic Md BT). Now click on **OK**.

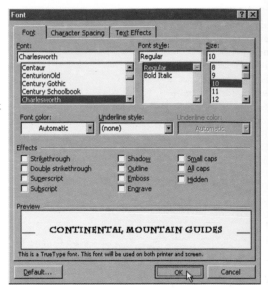

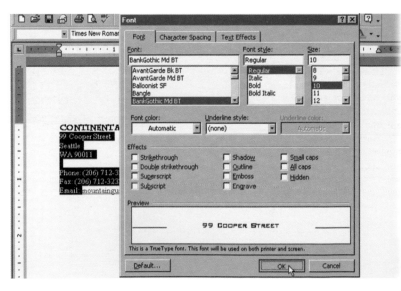

● The fonts have now been
changed, and the company
name, company address,
and email address are each
in a different font, which
distinguishes the various
elements from each other.

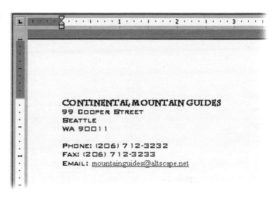

CHANGING THE FONT SIZE

Word's default font size of ten points
(a point is one seventy-second of an inch)
is fine for the bulk of the text that you

are likely to produce, but different parts of
your document, such as headings, can
benefit from being in a larger font size.

USING THE FONT SIZE SELECTOR BOX

● With the text that you
wish to resize already
highlighted (in this case the
company name), click on
the Font size selector box
in the Formatting toolbar,
scroll to 16 (meaning
16 point), and click on it.
The lettering of the selected
text is now larger.

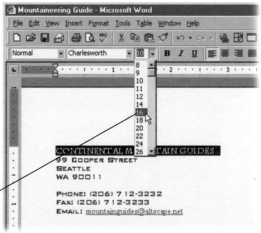

Selected font size ●

11 ㉖ Font size
selector

● Highlight the next three lines of the address and follow the same sequence to change the font size to 14 pt, and then do the same to change the final three lines to 12 pt. Your text should now appear as shown in this example.

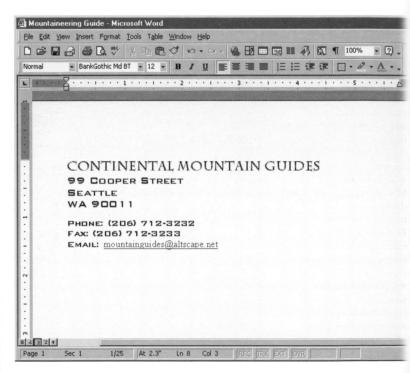

FONT STYLES

You will see that, as well as offering a choice of fonts, the **Font** dialog box also has a **Font style:** panel. Choosing different options in this panel will enable you to turn the font from its normal, or regular, form to italic, bold, or italic bold type, providing that all these variations are available in the particular font that you are using. These options can be used to emphasize parts of your text.

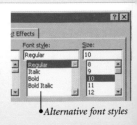

Alternative font styles

CHANGING THE FONT EFFECT

As well as bold, italic, and underline, there are a number of effects available in Word that you can use to change the appearance of your text. For example, shadowed, outlined, embossed, and engraved effects can all be used. Once you have followed this example, try out the other effects, some of which can be very useful.

EMBOSSING TEXT

● Begin by highlighting the company name in the address and open the **Font** dialog box ◻, and click on the **Font** tab at the top of the dialog box.

● In the center of the **Effects** section of the **Font** dialog box, you'll see check boxes for **Shadow**, **Outline**, **Emboss**, and **Engrave** effects. Click in the check box next to **Emboss** and then click on **OK**.

● Click anywhere on your page to remove the highlighting, and the embossed effect on the lettering becomes visible.

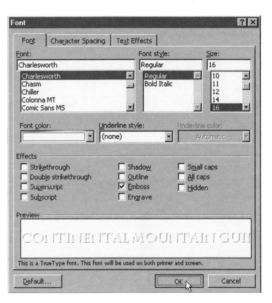

CONTINENTAL MOUNTAIN GUIDES

99 COOPER STREET
SEATTLE
WA 90011

PHONE: (206) 712-3232
FAX: (206) 712-3233
EMAIL: mountainguides@altscape.net

13 **Selecting a new font**

CHANGING THE LETTER SPACING

Changing the amount of space between individual letters can also be used to emphasize important parts of the text.

In this example, we will space out the letters of the company name to give it greater weight on the page.

INCREASING THE LETTER SPACING

● Highlight the company name again, open the **Font** dialog box ⬚, and click on the **Character Spacing** tab.

● In the **Spacing:** box, click on the arrow next to **Normal** and select **Expanded**. In the **By:** box, enter the figure **3**, meaning 3 pt, and click on **OK**.

● Click on the company name again to see how the name now extends across the page.

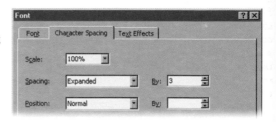

CHANGING THE FONT COLOR

With the increasing availability, and falling cost, of color printers, using some of the color options in Word offers a simple and effective way of making selected text stand out. Bear in mind that it's best not to combine too wide a range of colors.

1 SELECTING THE COLOR PALETTE

● Although the snowy-whiteness of the embossed text is appropriate for the company's business, it's a little pale. To change the font color, highlight the company name and then open the **Font** dialog box.
● Click the arrow to the right of the **Font color:** selection box and the color palette will appear.

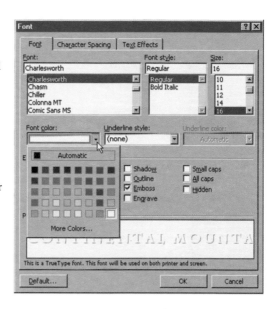

2 CHOOSING THE COLOR

● Move the mouse cursor down to **Blue** and click once. This color has now been selected for the text.

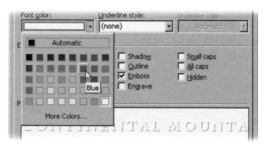

● The text in the **Preview** window now shows you the effect of the color change. If you are happy with this color, click on **OK**.

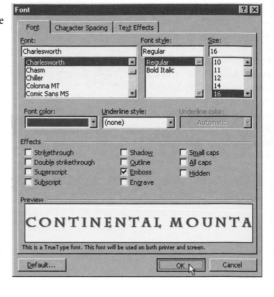

● Click anywhere on your page to remove the highlighting and reveal the text in the new color.

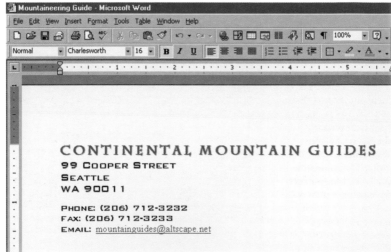

3 CHOOSING FURTHER COLORS

● As Word automatically colors the email address in blue, the contact details above the email address can also have their own colors. Try changing the **Phone:** details to orange and the **Fax:** line to sea green to achieve the effect shown in the example here.

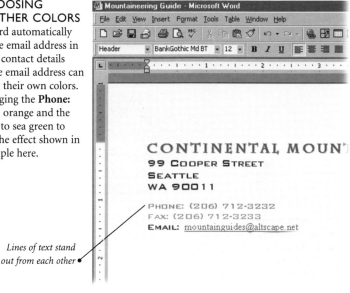

Lines of text stand out from each other ●

Bold, Italic, and Underline

The quickest way to change your text by using these effects is to highlight the text that you want to change and then click on one of these three buttons  in the Formatting toolbar. You're not limited to just one of these effects for a piece of text. You can have text that is bold and italic, as well as being underlined, if that's what you want.

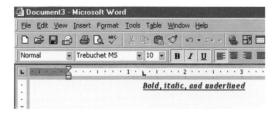

11 ㉗ Bold, ㉘ Italic, ㉙ Underline

STYLING PARAGRAPHS

As far as Word is concerned, a paragraph is any piece of text that ends with a paragraph mark, so the styling shown here can be applied to a single letter or to several pages of text.

ALIGNING PARAGRAPHS

There are four possible ways to align paragraphs in Word: left-aligned, centered, right-aligned, and justified. Left-alignment is the default paragraph alignment in Word. Each line of a paragraph starts against the left margin, and the line endings are "ragged" in the way a typewriter would produce them. Centered alignment has the effect of centering each line of a paragraph on the mid-point between the margins. Right-alignment has the effect of aligning the right-hand end of each line up against the right-hand margin leaving the start of each line ragged, and justified alignment produces a straight edge at both the beginning and the end of each line by adding spaces to make every line of text the same length.

1 SELECTING THE TEXT

● The company's details are going to be the heading of the guide, and a heading frequently benefits from having its own alignment, in order to distinguish it from the text on the rest of the page. Begin by highlighting all of the company's details.

CONTINENTAL MOUNTAIN GUIDES
99 COOPER STREET
SEATTLE
WA 90011
PHONE: (206) 712-3232
FAX: (206) 712-3233
EMAIL: mountainguides@altscape.net

2 ALIGNING TEXT TO THE RIGHT

● First we'll see how right-aligning affects the appearance, so click on the **Align Right** button  in the Formatting toolbar.

● Click off the highlighted text to see the effect.

● Although the shorter lines are obviously right-aligned, the company name has hardly moved because it almost fills the width of the page, and it sticks out way beyond the other lines.

Align Right

CONTINENTAL MOUNTAIN GUIDES
99 COOPER STREET
SEATTLE
WA 90011

PHONE: (206) 712-3232
FAX: (206) 712-3233
EMAIL: mountainguides@altscape.net

3 CENTERING THE TEXT

● The start of the company name looks as if it's out on a limb, so the whole heading would look better if it were centered.

● Highlight the company details again and click on the **Center** button  in the Formatting toolbar.

● Click off the highlighted text to see how the separate lines of the company's details now all appear to be part of a single unit.

Center

CONTINENTAL MOUNTAIN GUIDES
99 COOPER STREET
SEATTLE
WA 90011

PHONE: (206) 712-3232
FAX: (206) 712-3233
EMAIL: mountainguides@altscape.net

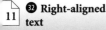
㉜ Right-aligned text

㉛ Centered text

INSERTING A DROPPED CAPITAL

First paragraphs can be made more noticeable by starting them with a large initial capital letter that drops down more than one line. This dropped capital letter is familiarly known as a "drop cap", and it is easily achieved in Word.

WHAT WE DO

Continental Mountain Guides has built up a fine reputation that now extends beyond the climbing community following two heavily publicized rescues that we were fortunate enough to be called to carry out. The expeditions we lead are always safe and successful, and one enthusiastic climber suggested out motto should be: "We ain't lost one yet." But as we never intend to, the suggestion was put to one side. We offer many climbing opportunities for the absolute beginner and to the climbing professional who might need our specialized knowledge of specific mountaineering regions. Guides join our staff when they have at least ten year's of climbing. And they have to demonstrate to us that they are dedicated to climbing and to sharing that passion.

1 SELECTING THE DROP CAP BOX

• The Mountaineering Guide has an introductory section with a heading that has been formatted in BankGothic Md BT 16 pt, and a paragraph formatted in Trebuchet MS 10 pt. This paragraph would be more interesting if it began with a drop cap.

• Place the cursor over the paragraph and click to position the insertion point within it. Go to **Format** in the Menu bar and select **Drop Cap**. The **Drop Cap** dialog box opens.

• Click on **Dropped** in the **Position** options.

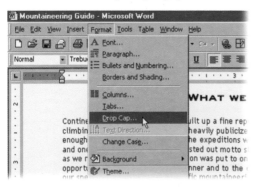

2 CHOOSING THE SIZE

● The **Lines to drop:** box shows the default number of lines for the capital letter to drop is **3**. This is too large a drop cap for a short paragraph, so change the figure to **2** and click on **OK**.

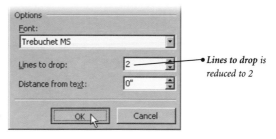

● *Lines to drop is reduced to 2*

● The drop cap is shown surrounded by a frame.

● Click elsewhere on the document and the altered paragraph, with its new dropped capital, appears as it will on the printed page.

ontinental Mounta
limbing communi
enough to be called to
and one enthusiastic
as we never intend to

Continental Mounta
climbing communi
enough to be called to
and one enthusiastic
as we never intend to

3 CREATING JUSTIFIED TEXT

● Finally, this paragraph would sit better with the company details above it if it were justified. Highlight the text and click on the **Justify** button in the Formatting toolbar.

● Both the beginnings and endings of the lines of the

ontinental Mounta
climbing commun
enough to be called to
and one enthusiastic
as we never intend to

paragraph now align, and the start of the document is beginning to look tidier.

OUNTAI

PER STREET

WHAT WE DO

Continental Mountain Guides has built up a fine reputation that now extends beyond the climbing community following two heavily publicized rescues that we were fortunate enough to be called to carry out. The expeditions we lead are always safe and successful, and one enthusiastic climber suggested out motto should be: "We ain't lost one yet." But as we never intend to, the suggestion was put to one side. We offer many climbing opportunities for the absolute beginner and to the climbing professional who might need our specialized knowledge of specific mountaineering regions. Guides join our staff when they have at least ten year's of climbing. And they have to demonstrate to us that they are dedicated to climbing and to sharing that passion.

11 ❸❸ **Justified text**

ADDING SPACE BETWEEN PARAGRAPHS

Creating space between paragraphs can improve the look of your document. This can be done by simply inserting a number of paragraph returns (Enter←). However, there is a better way of choosing precisely the amount of space you wish to insert.

1 SELECTING THE PARAGRAPH

● In a section of the Mountaineering Guide on seminars and expeditions, paragraphs are separated by paragraph marks (you can make these visible using the Standard toolbar ⁋).

● A better method of separating paragraphs, particularly when a large amount of space is required between them, is to select manually how much space there should be.

Extra paragraph returns add a fixed amount of space

● First delete the paragraph marks separating the paragraphs, and highlight the first paragraph. Then click on **Format** in the Menu bar and choose **Paragraph** from the menu.

· CLIMBING·SEMINARS¶
We·are·pleased·to·continue·to·offer·these·p
Alps.·You'll·spend·14·days·on·the·Gold·Rive
familiar·with·a·range·of·climbing·skills·inclu
belaying,·and·the·correct·use·of·ax·and·cra
glacier·travel·and·the·particular·rescue·me
intended·for·people·new·to·climbing·and,·b
skills·will·provide·a·sound·foundation·towar
¶
· TECHNICAL·CLIMBS¶
Guided·technical·climbs·are·undertaken·in·
glacier.·We·offer·these·and·others·each·sea
least·one·new·climb·before·the·end·of·each
climbers·only·because·they·can·be·physicall
party-size·for·safety·reasons,·which·means·
it·is·that·your·booking·will·be·successful.¶
¶
· EXPEDITION·SEMINARS¶
These·seminars·are·also·based·on·the·Gold·
and·concentrate·on·the·different·demands·

❷❶ **Show/hide formatting marks**

2 DEFINING THE SPACE

● The **Paragraph** dialog box opens. In the **Spacing** section, click on the up arrow in the **After:** panel. The entry now reads **6 pt** and the **Preview** panel shows the increased space following the paragraph. Click on **OK**.

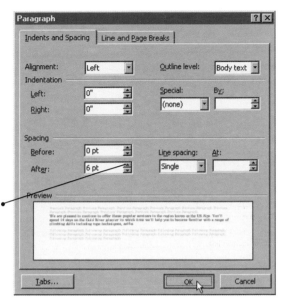

Up arrow increases the spacing after paragraph ●

● The paragraph is now separated from the following paragraph by a 6 pt space without an extra Enter↵ being inserted.

*Using the **Paragraph** formatting menu, this space can be made exactly the size you want it* ●

▪ CLIMBING SEMINARS¶
We·are·pleased·to·continue·to·offer·these·p
Alps.·You'll·spend·14·days·on·the·Gold·Rive
familiar·with·a·range·of·climbing·skills·inclu
belaying,·and·the·correct·use·of·ax·and·cra
glacier·travel·and·the·particular·rescue·me
intended·for·people·new·to·climbing·and,·b
skills·will·provide·a·sound·foundation·towar

▪ TECHNICAL CLIMBS¶
Guided·technical·climbs·are·undertaken·in·
glacier.·We·offer·these·and·others·each·se
least·one·new·climb·before·the·end·of·each
climbers·only·because·they·can·be·physical
party·size·for·safety·reasons,·which·means
it·is·that·your·booking·will·be·successful.¶

▪ EXPEDITION SEMINARS¶
These·seminars·are·also·based·on·the·Gold·
and·concentrate·on·the·different·demands·

CHANGING THE INDENT

In printing terms, a "displayed" paragraph is one where the beginning and ends of the lines are indented compared to the paragraphs before and after it, producing a narrower column of text. This has the effect of emphasizing the paragraph.

SETTING THE LEFT INDENT

● Highlight the first paragraph, about climbing seminars, and place the mouse cursor over the **Left Indent** box on the ruler.

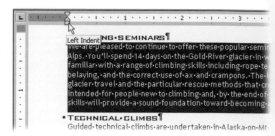

● Holding the mouse button down, drag the cursor to the right until the left indent box and the two indent arrows are over the quarter-inch mark, and release the mouse button. The left-hand edge of the paragraph is now indented.

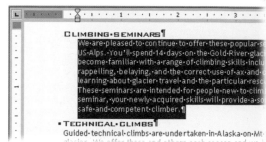

SETTING THE RIGHT INDENT

● Now place the mouse cursor over the right-hand indent arrow, hold down the mouse button, and drag the mouse cursor to the 5.5-inch position on the ruler and release the mouse button to set the indent.

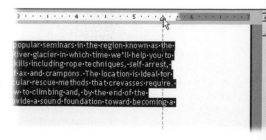

● The right-hand line
endings of the paragraph
are now indented.

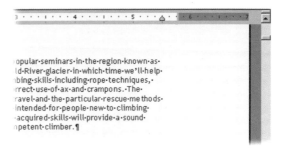

ADDING A BORDER

Word allows you to emphasize a selected
paragraph by adding a border in a range
of styles and colors. We are going to create
a border around the outside of the
selected text, but there are other options
available in the **Outside Border** menu.

1 OPENING THE BORDER MENU
● Highlight the paragraph
and click on the **Outside
Border** button in the
Formatting toolbar.

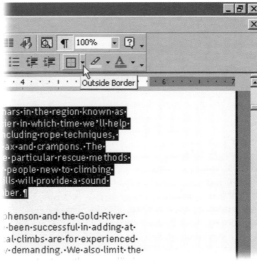

2 SELECTING OUTSIDE BORDER

● A menu of border selections appears. Click on the **Outside Border** option.

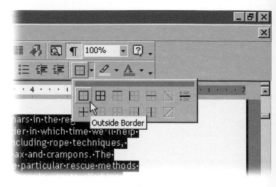

● The paragraph is now enclosed within a border.

CLIMBING·SEMINARS¶

We·are·pleased·to·continue·to·offer·these·popular·seminars·in·the·region·known·as· the·US·Alps.·You'll·spend·14·days·on·the·Gold·River·glacier·in·which·time·we'll·help· you·to·become·familiar·with·a·range·of·climbing·skills·including·rope·techniques,· self-arrest,·rappelling,·belaying,·and·the·correct·use·of·ax·and·crampons.·The· location·is·ideal·for·learning·about·glacier·travel·and·the·particular·rescue·methods· that·crevasses·require.·These·seminars·are·intended·for·people·new·to·climbing· and,·by·the·end·of·the·seminar,·your·newly·acquired·skills·will·provide·a·sound· foundation·toward·becoming·a·safe·and·competent·climber.¶

TECHNICAL·CLIMBS¶

3 CHANGING THE BORDER STYLE

● With the text within the border highlighted, go to the **Format** menu and click on **Borders and Shading**.

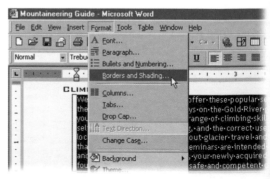

● The **Borders and Shading** dialog box opens. Click on the **Borders** tab if it is not already at the front. In the **Style:** panel, click on the down arrow and select one of the selection of borders by clicking on it. Click on **OK**.

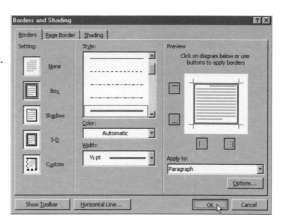

● The border around the paragraph changes to the selected style.

CLIMBING·SEMINARS¶

We·are·pleased·to·continue·to·offer·these·popular·seminars·in·the·region·known·as· the·US·Alps.·You'll·spend·14·days·on·the·Gold·River·glacier·in·which·time·we'll·help· you·to·become·familiar·with·a·range·of·climbing·skills·including·rope·techniques,· self-arrest,·rappelling,·belaying,·and·the·correct·use·of·ax·and·crampons.·The· location·is·ideal·for·learning·about·glacier·travel·and·the·particular·rescue·methods· that·crevasses·require.·These·seminars·are·intended·for·people·new·to·climbing· and,·by·the·end·of·the·seminar,·your·newly-acquired·skills·will·provide·a·sound· foundation·toward·becoming·a·safe·and·competent·climber.¶

TECHNICAL·CLIMBS¶

Guided·technical·climbs·are·undertaken·in·Alaska·on·Mt·Stephenson·and·the·Gold·River· glacier.·We·offer·these·and·others·each·season·and·we·have·been·successful·in·adding·at·

RESIZING BORDERS MANUALLY

There are two ways in which you can change the distance between the text and the border that encloses it. If you open the **Borders and Shading** dialog box you will see an **Options** button that allows the precise adjustment of the distance between the text and the border. An alternative method is simply to place the cursor against one of the sides of the border, hold down the mouse button, and drag the edge of the border to a new position.

4 ADDING COLOR TO THE BORDER

• With the text within the border highlighted, go to the Format menu and click on **Borders and Shading**. Click in the **Color:** box to display the color palette.

• Move the mouse cursor down and click on **Tan**.

• Click on **OK** and the border is now colored.

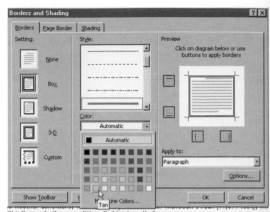

ill tell you whether expedition climbing is really for you.

CLIMBING·SEMINARS¶

We·are·pleased·to·continue·to·offer·these·popular·seminars·in·the·region·known·as· the·US·Alps.·You'll·spend·14·days·on·the·Gold·River·glacier·in·which·time·we'll·help· you·to·become·familiar·with·a·range·of·climbing·skills·including·rope·techniques,· self-arrest,·rappelling,·belaying,·and·the·correct·use·of·ax·and·crampons.·The· location·is·ideal·for·learning·about·glacier·travel·and·the·particular·rescue·methods· that·crevasses·require.·These·seminars·are·intended·for·people·new·to·climbing· and,·by·the·end·of·the·seminar,·your·newly·acquired·skills·will·provide·a·sound· foundation·toward·becoming·a·safe·and·competent·climber.¶

TECHNICAL·CLIMBS¶

REMOVING A BORDER

• With the text within the border highlighted, click on the **Outside Border** button in the Formatting toolbar. The menu of border selections appears.

• Move the mouse cursor over the **No Border** option and click to remove the border.

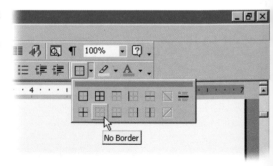

SHADING A PARAGRAPH

Whether or not a paragraph has been given a border, the text can be made to stand out by shading or coloring the background. Even if you don't have a color printer, this method can be used to choose a shade of gray, which can be effective.

1 SELECTING THE DIALOG BOX

● Highlight the paragraph, go to the Format menu in the toolbar and click on **Borders and Shading**. Now click on the **Shading** tab in the **Borders and Shading** dialog box to bring it to the foreground.

2 CHOOSING A COLOR

● Click on **Light Green** on the bottom row of the color palette, and the preview panel shows what this will look like.

● Click on **OK**, and the paragraph is now colored.

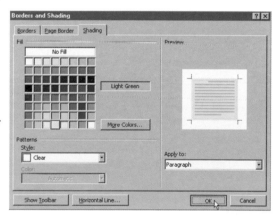

CLIMBING·SEMINARS¶

We·are·pleased·to·continue·to·offer·these·popular·seminars·in·the·region·known·as·the·US·Alps.·You'll·spend·14·days·on·the·Gold·River·glacier·in·which·time·we'll·help·you·to·become·familiar·with·a·range·of·climbing·skills·including·rope·techniques,·self-arrest,·rappelling,·belaying,·and·the·correct·use·of·ax·and·crampons.·The·location·is·ideal·for·learning·about·glacier·travel·and·the·particular·rescue·methods·that·crevasses·require.·These·seminars·are·intended·for·people·new·to·climbing·and,·by·the·end·of·the·seminar,·your·newly·acquired·skills·will·provide·a·sound·foundation·toward·becoming·a·safe·and·competent·climber.¶

TECHNICAL·CLIMBS¶

Guided·technical·climbs·are·undertaken·in·Alaska·on·Mt·Stephenson·and·the·Gold·River·glacier.·We·offer·these·and·others·each·season·and·we·have·been·successful·in·adding·at·

REMOVING SHADING FROM A PARAGRAPH

If you wish to remove shading that you have already created, follow these steps. With the paragraph highlighted, open the **Borders and Shading** dialog box via the Format menu, and choose **Shading**. Now click in the **No Fill** box above the color palette, click **OK**, and the shading is removed.

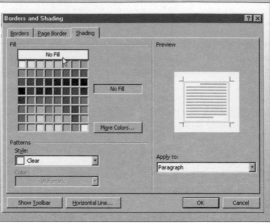

ALIGNING THE TEXT

● When text is within a rectangular border, it can look better being justified ◖. Highlight the paragraph and click on the **Justify** button in the Formatting toolbar. The text now fits neatly within the border.

CLIMBING SEMINARS¶

We are pleased to continue to offer these popular seminars in the region known as the US Alps. You'll spend 14 days on the Gold River glacier in which time we'll help you to become familiar with a range of climbing skills including rope techniques, self-arrest, rappelling, belaying, and the correct use of ax and crampons. The location is ideal for learning about glacier travel and the particular rescue methods that crevasses require. These seminars are intended for people new to climbing and, by the end of the seminar, your newly acquired skills will provide a sound foundation toward becoming a safe and competent climber.¶

TECHNICAL CLIMBS¶

USING FORMAT PAINTER

Once you've decided on a paragraph format that you want to apply to other paragraphs, you can apply the style by using a feature of Word known as **Format Painter**, rather than going through each individual step again for each paragraph.

1 SELECTING THE FORMAT TO COPY

● Select the paragraph whose format you wish to apply to another paragraph. Make sure that the paragraph mark is also selected. Click on the **Format Painter** button on the Standard toolbar ⌐.

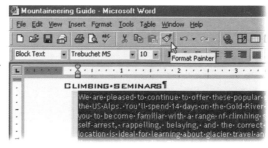

2 SELECTING THE NEW PARAGRAPH

● The cursor changes to a paintbrush icon. Move to the paragraph that is to be formatted in the same way as the selected paragraph.
● Click on the paragraph.

● All the formatting that has been done, including adding space, indenting the paragraph, adding a colored border and shading, and justifying the text, will be applied instantly to the chosen paragraph.

Formatting has been applied ●

MULTIPLE PAINTING

If you want to apply the same format to more than one paragraph by using **Format Painter**, double-click on the **Format Painter** button when you select it. You can then format as many paragraphs with the chosen format as you want by clicking in each one. When you've finished applying the format, either click on the **Format Painter** button to deselect or press the [Esc] key.

⑪ **Format painter**

LISTS AND COLUMNS

Some data looks neater and more readable when presented as a list or in a column. In this chapter we look at the list and column options available in Word, and how to use them.

NUMBERED LISTS

Displaying items line by line, each new entry starting with a number, is probably the most common form of list. Text that has already been typed in can be turned into a list, and Word also has the facility to create a list automatically as you type.

1 SELECT BULLETS AND NUMBERING

● Type in a list of items, starting a new line each time. Now highlight the list, go to the **Format** menu in the toolbar, and select **Bullets and Numbering**.

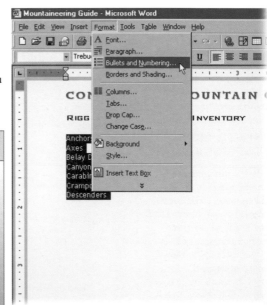

AUTOMATIC NUMBERING

Word detects when you are manually creating a numbered list. If you type a line of text that begins with a **1** followed by a space, when you press the [Enter ←] key, Word automatically begins the new line with a **2** and inserts a tab.

2 CHOOSING THE OPTION

● The **Bullets and Numbering** dialog box opens. Click on the **Numbered** tab to view the numbering options.

● Select the numbering style immediately to the right of the **None** box by clicking on that box. The chosen box is highlighted by a blue rectangle. Now click on **OK**.

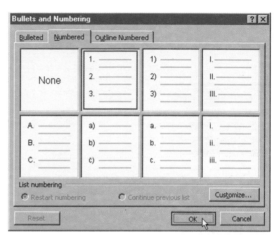

● The list of items is now numbered.

SWITCHING OFF THE NUMBERING

Word's automatic numbering feature can be annoying when you don't want to number every line. To remove a number, press the ⟨← Bksp⟩ backspace key once to delete the number, and again to remove the indent.

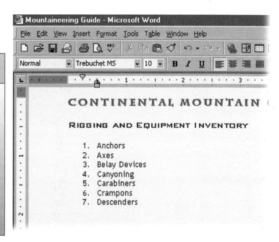

CHANGING THE INDENTS

As you have seen on the previous page, when you turn a list into a numbered list, Word automatically indents it. To remove the indent, or indent the list further, follow these steps. This method also works for other kinds of lists and for normal text.

1 SELECTING THE LIST
● If the list is not already highlighted, begin by doing so. Don't worry if the numbers themselves aren't highlighted. This is because Word treats them differently from regular text.

2 CHANGING THE INDENT
● Move the cursor up to the Formatting toolbar and click on the **Decrease Indent** button.

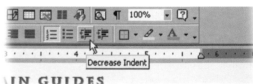

● The whole list moves to the left, aligning with the text above it.
● If you want to increase, rather than decrease, the indent, click on the **Increase Indent** button, which is to the right of the **Decrease Indent** button.

CONTINENTAL MOUNTAIN GUI

RIGGING AND EQUIPMENT INVENTORY

1. Anchors
2. Axes
3. Belay Devices
4. Canyoning
5. Carabiners
6. Crampons
7. Descenders

㊱ Decrease indent

㊲ Increase indent

BULLETED LISTS

Even when the lines in a list do not need to be numbered, you may still wish to emphasize the entries. Word offers a range of bulleted lists suited to different purposes. For example, you might use check marks for a list of completed tasks.

1 SELECTING THE LIST
● Begin by highlighting the list that you wish to bullet.
● Select **Bullets and Numbering** from the **Format** menu in the toolbar.

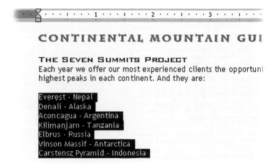

2 SELECTING THE BULLETED TAB
● In the **Bullets and Numbering** menu, click on the **Bulleted** tab to bring it to the front.

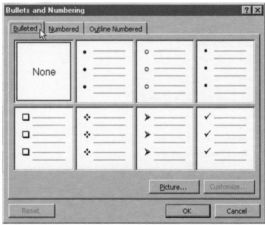

36 **Select bullets and numbering**

3 SELECTING THE BULLET STYLE

● There are several bullet styles that you can use, but in this example we are selecting the option next to **None**. Now click on **OK**.

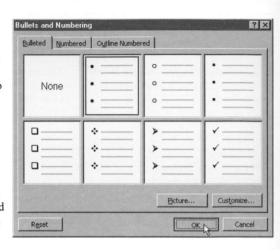

● The list now has a bullet at the start of each line, and you can change the indent, if you want to, as before.

PICTURE BULLETS

Word offers a very wide range of picture bullets. Click on **Picture** in the **Bulleted** tab of the **Bullets and Numbering** dialog box. A palette menu opens, and you can select a particular combination of shape and color from the variety available.

CONTINENTAL MOUNTAIN GUI

THE SEVEN SUMMITS PROJECT
Each year we offer our most experienced clients the opportuni highest peaks in each continent. And they are:

- Everest - Nepal
- Denali - Alaska
- Aconcagua - Argentina
- Kilimanjaro - Tanzania
- Elbrus - Russia
- Vinson Massif - Antarctica
- Carstensz Pyramid - Indonesia

QUICK LISTS

If you are happy with the default style of numbering or bullet size, there is a quick way to produce a numbered or bulleted list. Once you have typed in the list of items, highlight the list, and then click on either the Numbering button 🗋 or the Bullets button 🗋 in the Formatting toolbar.

 ❸❹ Numbered list 11

 ❸❺ Bulleted list 11

CREATING A TABBED LIST

Microsoft® Word includes the facility to set out text or figures in neat tables (see *Tables, Charts, And Graphs* in this series),

but for small amounts of information it can often be easier to create columns by turning the entries into a tabbed list.

1 INSERTING TABS BETWEEN ITEMS

● Type a list of items and press the [Tab↹] key between each item on each line. With the Formatting Marks turned on, the tab mark (the right-pointing arrow) shows where each tab has been inserted.

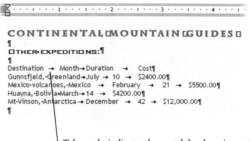

Tab marks indicate where a tab has been inserted

2 BRINGING UP THE TABS DIALOG BOX

● Take a look at the list and decide which is the longest left-hand entry. In this case it is the Mexican entry, at just over 1.5 inches wide.
● Ignoring the line of headings for the moment, highlight the rest of the list.
● Click on **Format** in the Menu bar, and choose **Tabs**.

3 SETTING A TAB STOP POSITION

● The **Tabs** dialog box opens. Given the length of the Mexico destination, we are going to set the first column at 2 inches, so in the **Tab stop position:** box type **2**. Now click on **Set**, and then click on **OK**.

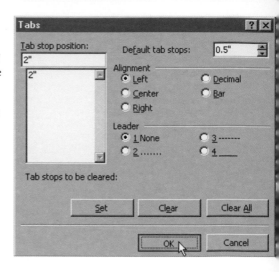

● A tab stop appears in the ruler at the 2-inch position, and the months are now lined up in a column.

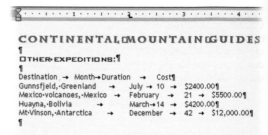

4 SETTING THE NEXT TAB STOP

● With the list still highlighted, follow the same steps to set another tab at 3 inches. The numbers of the duration are now lined up.

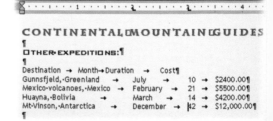

5 SETTING A DECIMAL TAB

● So far we've only used a left tab, that is, the items are lined up down their left-hand side. The cost figures would look better lined up down their right-hand side, so we will use a decimal tab.

● With the list highlighted, open the **Tabs** dialog box again. Set a tab at 4 inches and click on the **Decimal** radio button.

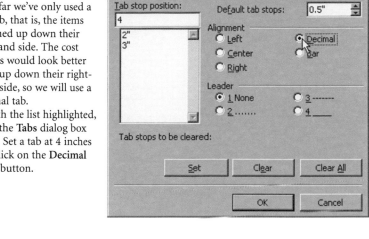

● Click on **Set** and then on **OK**. A decimal tab stop appears on the ruler, and the prices are now aligned down the decimal point at the 4-inch position.

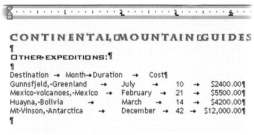

REMOVING A TAB SETTING FROM THE RULER

A quick way to remove a tab setting is first to highlight the text that contains the tab. Place the mouse cursor on the ruler tab setting that you want to remove, and hold the mouse button down. The vertical alignment line appears, but all you need to do is to drag the tab symbol down off the ruler and release the mouse button. The tab disappears.

SETTING TABS BY THE RULER

As is the case with many of the functions in Microsoft® Word, there is more than one way of setting tabs. Using the ruler provides a more visual method than the **Tabs** dialog box, and allows you to make quick adjustments until you are satisfied.

1 SETTING THE FIRST TAB IN THE RULER

• The headings above the list still need aligning over their respective columns. Highlight that line and click on the ruler at the 2-inch mark. A left tab appears on the ruler.

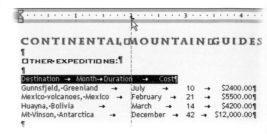

• The **Destination** heading remains aligned to the left, but the **Month** heading now lines up with the months below it.

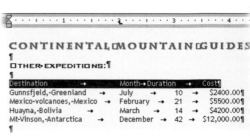

2 SELECTING A CENTER TAB

• With the line of headings still highlighted, click on the **Left Tab** symbol at the left-hand end of the ruler. The symbol for a **Center Tab** appears. This tab has the effect of centering text on the tab.

3 SETTING THE CENTER TAB

● Click on the ruler at the 3-inch mark. A center tab is set and the word **Duration** is almost centered above the list of days.

```
CONTINENTAL MOUNTAIN GUIDES
¶
OTHER·EXPEDITIONS:¶
¶
Destination          →        Month →  Duration → Cost¶
Gunnsfjeld,·Greenland    →     July    →    10   →   $2400.00¶
Mexico·volcanoes,·Mexico  →   February →  21   →   $5500.00¶
Huayna,·Bolivia       →        March   →   14   →   $4200.00¶
Mt·Vinson,·Antarctica   →      December →  42   →   $12,000.00¶
¶
```

4 FINE TUNING THE SETTING

● The word **Duration** is slightly to the left of center, so move the cursor up to the ruler, place it over the center tab and hold down the mouse button. A dotted vertical alignment line now appears down the screen. Move the cursor slightly to the right until this line falls exactly between the digits.

● Release the mouse button, and the heading is now precisely centered over the column of numbers.

```
CONTINENTAL MOUNTAIN GUIDES
¶
OTHER·EXPEDITIONS:¶
¶
Destination          →        Month →  Duration → Cost¶
Gunnsfjeld,·Greenland    →     July    →    10   →   $2400.00¶
Mexico·volcanoes,·Mexico  →   February →  21   →   $5500.00¶
Huayna,·Bolivia       →        March   →   14   →   $4200.00¶
Mt·Vinson,·Antarctica   →      December →  42   →   $12,000.00¶
¶
```

```
CONTINENTAL MOUNTAIN GUIDES
¶
OTHER·EXPEDITIONS:¶
¶
Destination          →        Month →  Duration → Cost¶
Gunnsfjeld,·Greenland    →     July    →    10   →   $2400.00¶
Mexico·volcanoes,·Mexico  →   February →  21   →   $5500.00¶
Huayna,·Bolivia       →        March   →   14   →   $4200.00¶
Mt·Vinson,·Antarctica   →      December →  42   →   $12,000.00¶
¶
```

5 SELECTING A RIGHT TAB

● Finally, click through the options of the tab button at the left-hand end of the ruler until the **Right Tab** symbol appears.

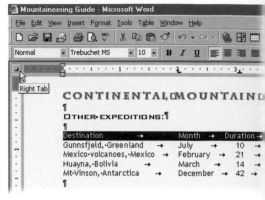

6 SETTING THE RIGHT TAB

● Click on the ruler at about the 4.2-inch mark. The end of the word **Cost** is now aligned with the trailing zeroes of the amounts in the column.

7 CHECKING THE EFFECT

● The right tab lines up the right-hand end of the text. To see the effect, change **Cost** to **Cost/person**. The words move to the left as you type, and the end of "person" is aligned with the zeroes. The effect is clearer with the formatting marks turned off ⬏.

CONTINENTAL MOUNTAIN GUIDES

OTHER EXPEDITIONS:

Destination	Month	Duration	Cost/person
Gunnsfjeld, Greenland	July	10	$2400.00
Mexico volcanoes, Mexico	February	21	$5500.00
Huayna, Bolivia	March	14	$4200.00
Mt Vinson, Antarctica	December	42	$12,000.00

 26 Selecting the paragraph

---

8 ADDING LEADERS BETWEEN ITEMS

● One way of making it easier to read across tabbed columns is to add a leader between each one.

● Highlight the list of destinations and click on **Tabs** in the **Format** menu. The **Tabs** dialog box opens. Click on the radio button next to **2.......**, and then click on **Set**.

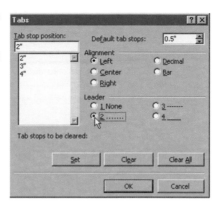

● Now highlight 3" in the **Tab stop position:** list of tabs, click on the radio button next to **2.......** again, and then click on **Set**.

● Repeat this process for the 4" tab position and click on **OK**. The list of expeditions now has rows of leaders to make the list more readable.

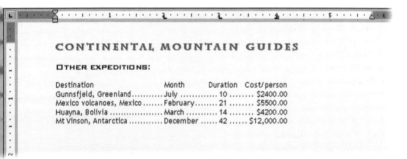

CONTINENTAL MOUNTAIN GUIDES

OTHER EXPEDITIONS:

Destination	Month	Duration	Cost/person
Gunnsfjeld, Greenland	July	10	$2400.00
Mexico volcanoes, Mexico	February	21	$5500.00
Huayna, Bolivia	March	14	$4200.00
Mt Vinson, Antarctica	December	42	$12,000.00

USING MULTIPLE COLUMNS

We have looked at ways of turning lists into columns, but there are times when continuous text benefits from being set in columns, too. This can give the page a newspaper like appearance, and can be useful in newsletters and pamphlets.

1 CHOOSING THE COLUMNS OPTION

● In this example, the Mountain Guides brochure includes a section on rented accommodation, which we are going to set in columns.

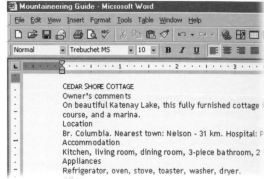

● Begin by highlighting the text that you want to be laid out in columns.
● Then click on **Format** in the Menu bar and choose **Columns** from the drop-down menu.

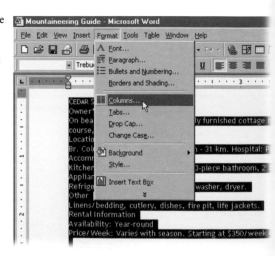

2 SET THE NUMBER OF COLUMNS

● The **Columns** dialog box opens. Click on box **Three** in the **Presets** section of the dialog box to select three columns, and click on **OK**.

● The preview panel shows how the text will look.

● Click on **OK**, and the selected text is now set out in three columns, with the default space of 0.5 inches between them.

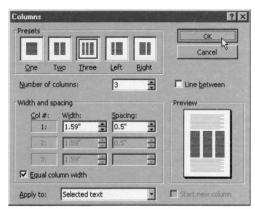

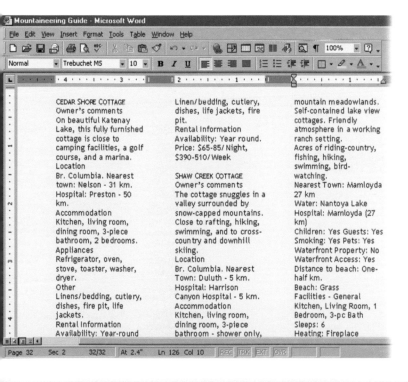

CEDAR SHORE COTTAGE
Owner's comments
On beautiful Katenay Lake, this fully furnished cottage is close to camping facilities, a golf course, and a marina.
Location
Br. Columbia. Nearest town: Nelson - 31 km. Hospital: Preston - 50 km.
Accommodation
Kitchen, living room, dining room, 3-piece bathroom, 2 bedrooms.
Appliances
Refrigerator, oven, stove, toaster, washer, dryer.
Other
Linens/bedding, cutlery, dishes, fire pit, life jackets.
Rental Information
Availability: Year-round

Linen/bedding, cutlery, dishes, life jackets, fire pit.
Rental Information
Availability: Year round.
Price: $65-85/ Night, $390-510/ Week

SHAW CREEK COTTAGE
Owner's comments
The cottage snuggles in a valley surrounded by snow-capped mountains. Close to rafting, hiking, swimming, and to cross-country and downhill skiing.
Location
Br. Columbia. Nearest Town: Duluth - 5 km. Hospital: Harrison Canyon Hospital - 5 km.
Accommodation
Kitchen, living room, dining room, 3-piece bathroom - shower only,

mountain meadowlands. Self-contained lake view cottages. Friendly atmosphere in a working ranch setting.
Acres of riding-country, fishing, hiking, swimming, bird-watching.
Nearest Town: Mamloyda 27 km
Water: Nantoya Lake
Hospital: Mamloyda (27 km)
Children: Yes Guests: Yes
Smoking: Yes Pets: Yes
Waterfront Property: No
Waterfront Access: Yes
Distance to beach: One-half km.
Beach: Grass
Facilities - General
Kitchen, Living Room, 1 Bedroom, 3-pc Bath
Sleeps: 6
Heating: Fireplace

3 INSERTING COLUMN BREAKS

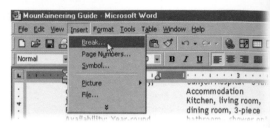

• The information would be clearer if each column began with a new entry. This can be done by using column breaks.

• Place the cursor at the point in the text where you would like to start a new column, click on **Insert** in the **Menu** bar, and choose **Break** from the menu.

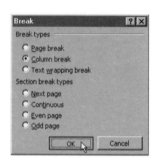

• The **Break** dialog box opens. Click on the radio button next to **Column break** and click on **OK**.

• By using this method, each column can begin with a new entry.

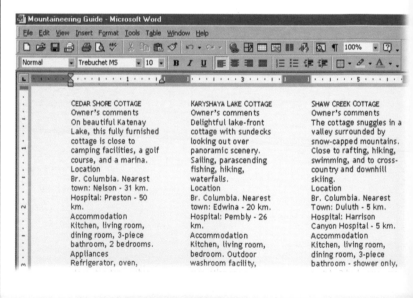

CEDAR SHORE COTTAGE
Owner's comments
On beautiful Katenay Lake, this fully furnished cottage is close to camping facilities, a golf course, and a marina.
Location
Br. Columbia. Nearest town: Nelson - 31 km. Hospital: Preston - 50 km.
Accommodation
Kitchen, living room, dining room, 3-piece bathroom, 2 bedrooms.
Appliances
Refrigerator, oven,

KARYSHAYA LAKE COTTAGE
Owner's comments
Delightful lake-front cottage with sundecks looking out over panoramic scenery. Sailing, parascending fishing, hiking, waterfalls.
Location
Br. Columbia. Nearest town: Edwina - 20 km. Hospital: Pembly - 26 km.
Accommodation
Kitchen, living room, bedroom. Outdoor washroom facility,

SHAW CREEK COTTAGE
Owner's comments
The cottage snuggles in a valley surrounded by snow-capped mountains. Close to rafting, hiking, swimming, and to cross-country and downhill skiing.
Location
Br. Columbia. Nearest Town: Duluth - 5 km. Hospital: Harrison Canyon Hospital - 5 km.
Accommodation
Kitchen, living room, dining room, 3-piece bathroom - shower only,

4 INSERTING VERTICAL LINES

● Rather than having blank spaces between columns, you can insert a vertical line between them. Place the cursor anywhere in the columns, open the **Columns** dialog box ⌐, and click in the **Line between** check box.

● Click on **OK** and the columns are now separated by a vertical line, which helps lead the eye in the same way that we saw earlier with tab leaders ⌐.

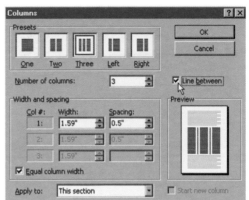

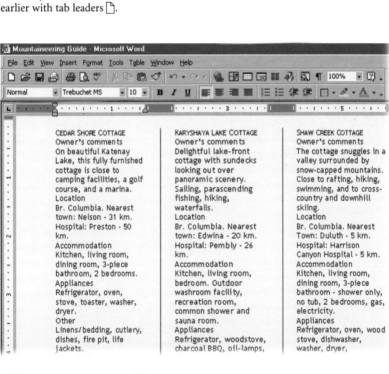

CEDAR SHORE COTTAGE
Owner's comments
On beautiful Katenay Lake, this fully furnished cottage is close to camping facilities, a golf course, and a marina.
Location
Br. Columbia. Nearest town: Nelson - 31 km. Hospital: Preston - 50 km.
Accommodation
Kitchen, living room, dining room, 3-piece bathroom, 2 bedrooms.
Appliances
Refrigerator, oven, stove, toaster, washer, dryer.
Other
Linens/bedding, cutlery, dishes, fire pit, life jackets.

KARYSHAYA LAKE COTTAGE
Owner's comments
Delightful lake-front cottage with sundecks looking out over panoramic scenery. Sailing, parascending fishing, hiking, waterfalls.
Location
Br. Columbia. Nearest town: Edwina - 20 km. Hospital: Pembly - 26 km.
Accommodation
Kitchen, living room, bedroom. Outdoor washroom facility, recreation room, common shower and sauna room.
Appliances
Refrigerator, woodstove, charcoal BBQ, oil-lamps,

SHAW CREEK COTTAGE
Owner's comments
The cottage snuggles in a valley surrounded by snow-capped mountains. Close to rafting, hiking, swimming, and to cross-country and downhill skiing.
Location
Br. Columbia. Nearest Town: Duluth - 5 km. Hospital: Harrison Canyon Hospital - 5 km.
Accommodation
Kitchen, living room, dining room, 3-piece bathroom - shower only, no tub, 2 bedrooms, gas, electricity.
Appliances
Refrigerator, oven, wood stove, dishwasher, washer, dryer,

48 Choosing the columns option

47 Adding leaders between items

USING STYLE SHEETS

This chapter deals with style sheets, a feature of Word that enables you to define many aspects of the style of each kind of text and apply the defined styles throughout your document.

THE POWER OF THE STYLE SHEET

Style sheets are one of the most powerful – and least understood – features of Word. Each style sheet is a list of formatting instructions, or styles, that can be applied to text. Every document is based on a style sheet. When you open a new document by clicking on the **New Blank Document** button in the Standard toolbar, Word automatically bases it on the normal style sheet, which is why the word **Normal** appears in the **Style** box at the end of the Formatting toolbar.

DEFINING FEATURES

A style sheet can define many features of a section of text. These include the font, and its size, color, and effects; the shape of a paragraph as determined by indents, spacing, and how page breaks are controlled; the position and alignment of tabs; what borders and shading are used, if any; and how bullets and numbering are styled. The smallest unit to which a style sheet can be applied is a paragraph, which need only be one line that ends with a paragraph mark.

CHOOSING ELEMENTS

To apply styles sensibly to a document, first identify the various parts of the text that play different roles. For example in a book, the title, the table of contents, main text, captions, and index all play different roles, and can all be styled differently. The styles can be set in separate style sheets and applied.

SAVING TIME

Once a style sheet has been created, any changes that you make to that sheet are automatically applied to all parts of your document that are based on that style.

`··4····|····3····|`

CEDAR SHORE COTTAGE

Owner's comments
On beautiful Katenay Lake, this fully furnished cottage is close to camping facilities, a golf course, and a marina.

Location
Br. Columbia. Nearest town: Nelson - 31 km. Hospital: Preston - 50 km.

Accommodation
Kitchen, living room, dining room, 2 piece

Styled text •
Using a style sheet, a defined font, type size, and indent has been applied to every instance of this kind of text each time it appears in the document.

CREATING A NEW STYLE SHEET

Style Sheets come into their own when applied to a document in which the information falls into various categories, and in which these categories are used

repeatedly. In the example below, each entry in the directory contains the same categories of information, such as **Owner's comments**, **Location**, and **Accommodation**.

1 SELECTING THE TEXT

• The list of cabins and their details has all been formatted in Trebuchet 10 pt. Now, new styles are going to be designed for each part of the details of the properties, starting with the name of the property.
• Highlight the name of the first property and click on **Format** in the **Menu** bar. Now click on **Style** in the drop-down menu.

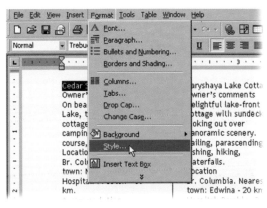

2 OPENING A NEW STYLE OPTION

• The **Style** dialog box opens. Click on **New** to create a new style for the property name. The text that you have highlighted can be seen in the preview box, and this will show the effects of any changes that you make to its style.

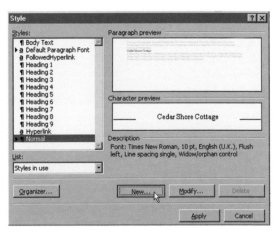

3 NAMING THE STYLE

• The **New Style** dialog box now opens. The first task is to give a name to the new style that we are creating, so type **Property Name** in the **Name:** box. A descriptive name like this will help you to know which style to choose when you are styling text at a later date.

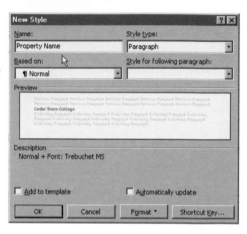

4 CHOOSING THE FONT

• Now click on **Format** at the bottom of the **New Style** dialog box, and click on **Font** in the pop-up menu.

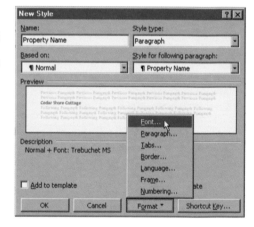

• The **Font** dialog box
opens. This box offers you
a range of possibilities for
changing the appearance of
the font, including the font
itself, its style (Italic etc.),
and its size.

• In the **Font:** selection box
choose BankGothic Md BT,
and you will see that the
text is now shown in this
font in the preview panel.

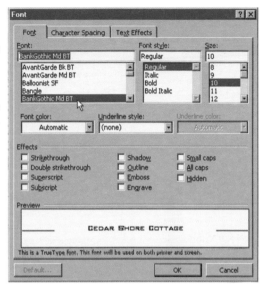

5 CHANGING THE FONT SIZE

• In the **Size:** selection box
choose **14**. Again, the text
in the preview panel now
reflects this change.

• BankGothic Md BT is an upper-case only font, that is, it does not use lower-case letters. However, if you are using a font that is upper- and lower-case, click the **Small caps** check box of the **Effects** section. This has the effect of turning all the lower-case letters into small capital letters.

• Click on **OK**.

6 INTRODUCING SPACE AFTER

• The appearance of the text on the page would be improved if there were a small space between the name and the text that follows it.

• Click on **Format** in the **New Style** dialog box and then click on **Paragraph** in the pop-up menu.

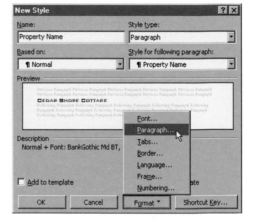

● The **Paragraph** dialog box opens. In the **Spacing** section, click once on the up arrow to the right of the **After:** box. The figure of **six pt** appears in the panel, meaning that a 6 point space will be inserted after the property name.
● Click on **OK** to close the **Paragraph** dialog box.

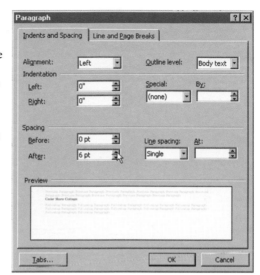

● The **New Style** dialog box now reappears. In the **Description** box the new formatting that has been chosen is shown.
● Click on **OK** to close the **New Style** dialog box and save this new style.

7 APPLYING THE NEW STYLE

● Click on **Apply** in the **Style** box, which is now visible again.

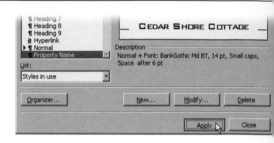

● The new style is now applied to the name of the property.

8 CREATING ANOTHER STYLE

● The details of each property are divided into sections, and a style is needed for the section heads. Highlight the words **Owner's comments**. Choose **Style** from the **Format** menu and click on **New** to open the **New Style** dialog box. Call this style **Section Head**.

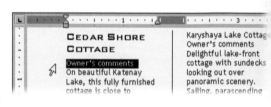

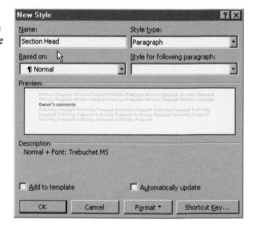

CREATING A NEW STYLE SHEET · 59

• Click on **Format** and
again click on **Font** to open
the **Font:** dialog box.
• Choose **Californian FB**
as the font and choose **Bold**
in the **Font style:** box. Click
on **OK**.

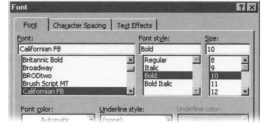

• The **New Style** dialog
box reappears. Click on
Format, select **Paragraph** to
open the **Paragraph** dialog
box, and in the **Spacing
After:** box type **2**. This will
introduce a small space
after the heading. Click on
OK to close the **Paragraph**
dialog box.

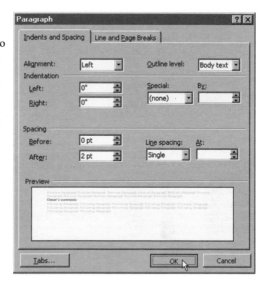

• Click on **OK** in the **New
Style** dialog box and click
on **Apply** in the **Style**
dialog box. The section
heading now has the
required style.

9 STYLING THE MAIN TEXT

● The text of each section needs its own style. Click in the paragraph below the newly styled **Owner's comments**, select **Style** from the **Format** menu, click on **New** to open the **New Style** dialog box, and call this style **Section Details**.

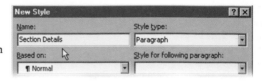

● Click on **Format** and select **Font** to open the **Font** dialog box. This time choose **Trebuchet MS** and make it 9 pt. Click on **OK** to return to the **New Style** box.

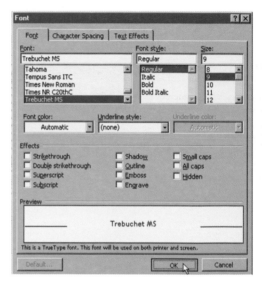

INDENTING THE TEXT

● The text will stand out more if it is indented. From the **Format** pop-up menu choose **Paragraph** and in the **Indentation** section of the **Paragraph** dialog box click on the up arrow of the **Left:** box. The figure of **0.1"** appears. Click on **OK**.

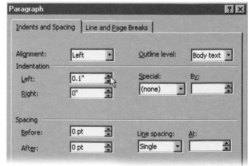

● Click **OK** again in the **New Style** box, click on **Apply**, and the text that appears, in the chosen font, is indented.

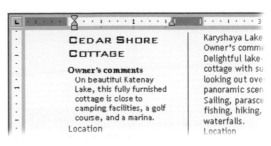

APPLYING YOUR STYLE SHEETS

● Highlight the name of the second property at the top of the second column.

● Click on the down arrow to the right of the **Style** selection box and move the cursor down to **Property Name**. (The other styles in the **Style** menu shown here may not be identical to the list in your **Style** menu.)

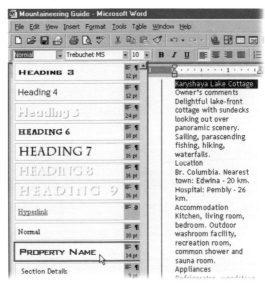

● Click on **Property Name** and that style is applied to the second property name.

• Highlight **Owner's comments** beneath it and select the **Section Head** style.

• Click on **Section Head** and the style is applied to the heading.

Text now changes to Section Head style •

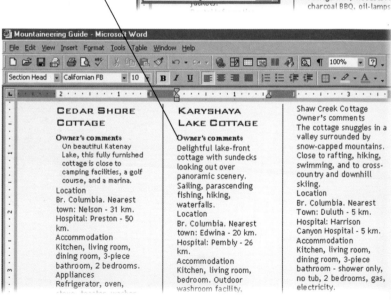

● Highlight the text beneath that heading and from the style list select **Section Details**. Click on **Section Details** and the style is applied to the highlighted text.

● Follow these steps to apply the style sheets to all the text throughout your document.

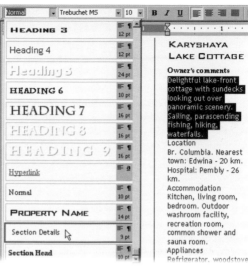

Text now changes to Section Details style ●

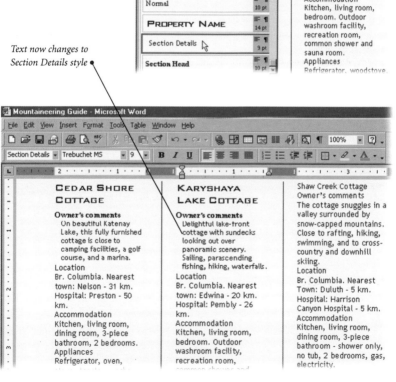

USING FORMAT PAINTER TO APPLY STYLES

We have seen how to create style sheets and apply them to all the text throughout a document, but this last process can be laborious if the text is extensive. Luckily, Word offers a solution – Format Painter enables you to do the job much faster.

1 STYLING THE PROPERTY NAME

● Highlight the property name at the top of the second column and make sure that you include the paragraph mark because this contains all the style details for the paragraph. (You can turn on the Formatting Marks to ensure that the paragraph mark is highlighted.)
● Click on the **Format Painter** icon in the Standard toolbar.
● Your cursor now has a paintbrush icon next to it. Go to the property name at the top of the third column and highlight it.

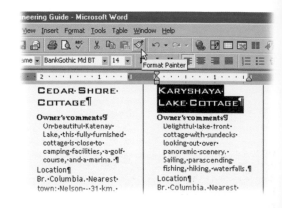

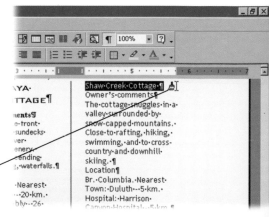

Paintbrush icon

10 ㉑ Show/hide formatting marks

10 ⑪ Format painter

● Release the mouse button, and the text is now styled in the selected style.

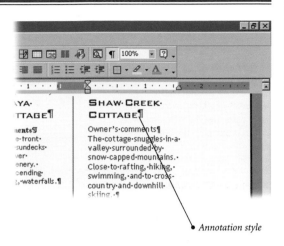

Annotation style

2 STYLING THE SECTION HEAD

● Select **Owner's comments** near the top of the first paragraph and double-click on the **Format Painter** button. You can now "paint" all the section heads in the text with the **Section Head** style 🔖. Press the ESC key, or click on the **Format Painter** button again when you have produced this result.

Styled Section Head ●

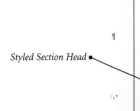

Multiple painting

3 STYLING THE SECTION DETAILS

• Finally, highlight the first paragraph in the first column that has been formatted with the **Section Details** style, double-click on the **Format Painter** button and apply the style to all the remaining unstyled paragraphs.

• The document should now look like the one below, with all text in the chosen styles.

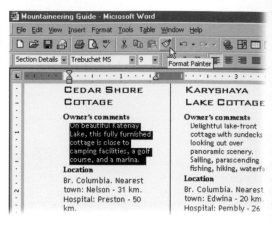

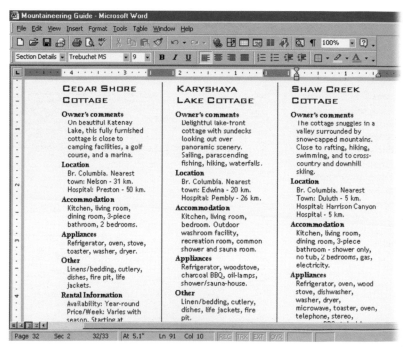

MAKING ONE STYLE FOLLOW ANOTHER

Once you have decided that one style is always to be followed by a second particular style, you can instruct Word always to follow the first style with the second. Begin by clicking on **Format** in the **Menu** bar and selecting **Style** to open the **Style** dialog box.

1 SELECTING THE FIRST STYLE

● In the **Style** dialog box, select the first of the two styles, in this case **Section Head**, and click on **Modify**.

Chosen style

2 SELECTING THE SECOND STYLE

● The **Modify Style** dialog box opens. The first style, **Section Head**, appears in the **Name:** box. Click on the down arrow to the right of the **Style for following paragraph:** box to drop down the list of styles.
● Click on the style that is to follow the first style, in this case **Section Details**.

Modify Style ?×

Name:
Section Head

Style type:
Paragraph

Based on:
¶ Normal

Style for following paragraph:
¶ Section Head
¶ Note Heading
¶ Plain Text
¶ Property Name
¶ Salutation
¶ Section Details
¶ Section Head

Preview

Previous Paragraph Previous Paragraph Previous Paragraph Previous Paragraph Previous Paragraph Previous Paragraph
Previous Paragraph
Accommodation
Following Paragraph Following Paragraph Following Paragraph Following Paragraph Following Paragraph Following Paragraph Following Paragraph

Description
Normal + Font: Californian FB, Bold, Space after 2 pt

☐ Add to template   ☐ Automatically update

OK   Cancel   Format ▾   Shortcut Key...

3 SAVING THE CHANGES

● **Section Details** appears in the **Style for following paragraph:** box.

● Click on **OK**, and the **Modify Style** dialog box closes. Now click on **Close** in the **Style** dialog box to complete the changes.

● On each occasion now when **Section Head** is used as a style and the [Enter ←] key is pressed, the following text will be formatted with the **Section Details** style.

STYLING FROM A TEXT SELECTION

So far we have created styles by choosing each of the features for the style through the **Style** dialog box. An alternative method is to begin by formatting a paragraph with all the style features that you want to be in a style sheet.

1 FORMATTING THE TEXT

● In this example, the following formatting has been applied to the text:
Font: *Gill Sans Ultra Bold*
Font size: *16 pt*
Font color: *Red*
Space after: *12 pt*
Border setting: *Shadow*
Border style: *Thin-thick*
Border color: *Tan*
Shading: *Light Yellow*
Text: *Centered*
Right indent: *3.77 inches*

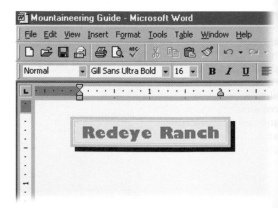

2 FROM A FORMAT TO A STYLE

● Highlight the text that you have formatted, click on **Format** in the **Menu** bar, select **Style** to open the **Style** box, and click on **New** near the foot of the dialog box to open the **New Style** dialog box. Word has picked up the formatting specifications of the selected text and almost all of them are shown in the **Description** section of this dialog box. Certain elements are not shown only because the **Description** box is too small to contain them all. Enter a name for the new style (here the name **Redeye** has been chosen). Click on **OK** to close the **New Style** dialog box.

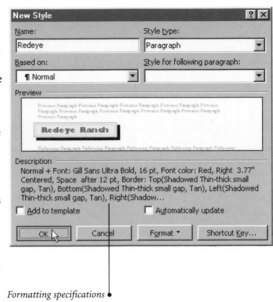

Formatting specifications

3 MAKING THE STYLE AVAILABLE

● The **Style** dialog box reappears with the new style listed in the **Style** menu to the left. To close the dialog box, just click on **Apply** even though the text already contains the required formatting. This style is now available to be applied quickly to any chosen text.

GLOSSARY

ALIGNMENT
In word processing, this refers to the side of the text that is aligned in a straight vertical line along one side (for instance, left-aligned text is straight on the left side and the ends of the lines are ragged on the right).

BORDER
A decorative effect that can be applied to surround any amount of text that ends with a paragraph mark.

CENTERED TEXT
One or more lines of text that are laid out on the page centered around the midpoint of the text area of a document.

COLUMN BREAK
A manually inserted break to end one column and force the text to start at the beginning of the next column.

COPY
To copy part of the text so that the same piece of text can be "pasted" into a new position (in the same document or another document) without removing the original piece of text.

CUT
To remove a block of text, in order to remove it permanently or to "paste" into a new position (in the same document or another document).

DIALOG BOX
A rectangle that appears on the screen and prompts you for a reply, usually with buttons, such as OK or Cancel.

DROP CAP (CAPITAL)
An initial letter of a paragraph that is larger than the rest of the text of the paragraph and that drops down two or more lines.

FONT EFFECT
A number of effects that can be applied to text, such as shadows, embossing, and engraving, and that are in addition to the type of font and its size.

FORMAT PAINTER
A method of applying an existing character and paragraph format to another part of the document.

INDENT
The indent shifts part of the text, or just the first line in every paragraph, across the screen.

JUSTIFIED TEXT
Text that is aligned to both left and right sides, so there is no ragged edge either side.

LETTER SPACING
The gap between letters that are next to one another, which can be altered by increasing or decreasing it.

MARGIN
The distance between the text and the paper edge. There are four margins on a page: top, bottom, left, and right.

PASTE
To put text that has been "cut" or "copied" back into the document at the insertion point.

RULER
Indicators at the top and left of the screen, with marks in inches or centimeters like a real ruler. Rulers also show the indents and margins of the text.

SCROLL BARS
Bars at the foot and the right of the screen that can be used to scroll around the document. The vertical one (on the right) is the more useful.

SHADING
Also known as a "Fill", this effect applies a background color or shade to a section of selected text.

STYLE SHEET
A collection of formatting instructions covering a wide range of possible styles and layouts that can all be applied simultaneously to a selected area of text.

TAB LEADERS
A sequence of periods or hyphens leading from the end of a section of text to the text at the next tab position. These lead the eye, such as in a table of contents where they are sometimes found between the end of a chapter title and the page on which it begins.

TABS
Preset or customized positions along one or more lines of text. Text will be aligned down the page against these positions when the tab position is reached after pressing the tab key.

INDEX

ACKNOWLEDGMENTS

PUBLISHER'S ACKNOWLEDGMENTS
Dorling Kindersley would like to thank the following:
Paul Mattock of APM, Brighton, for commissioned photography.
Microsoft Corporation for permission to reproduce screens
from within Microsoft® Word 2000.

Every effort has been made to trace the copyright holders.
The publisher apologizes for any unintentional omissions and would be pleased,
in such cases, to place an acknowledgment in future editions of this book.

Microsoft® is a registered trademark of Microsoft Corporation
in the United States and/or other countries.